JN126453

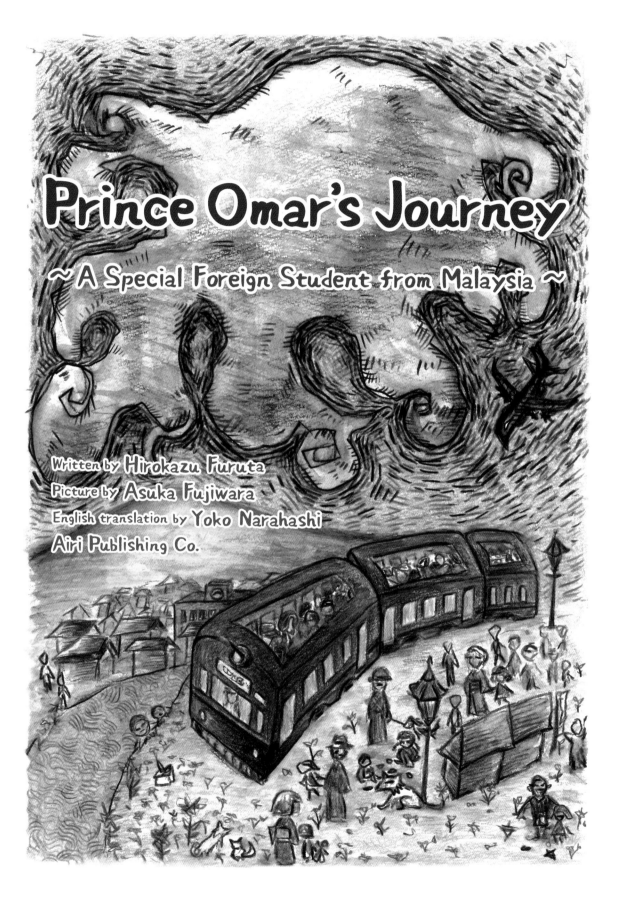

Prince Omar's Journey

~ A Special Foreign Student from Malaysia ~

Written by Hirokazu Furuta
Picture by Asuka Fujiwara
English translation by Yoko Narahashi
Airi Publishing Co.

I lived here ....

My name is Said Omar.

I was born in Malaysia and raised in a
Malaysian Royal family. I came to Japan as a
"special student from the south" in 1943
towards the end of World War II.

The Japanese people welcomed
foreign students very warmly.

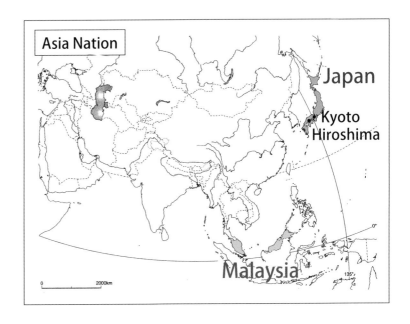

Happy days in Hiroshima

I enjoyed them !

【From the papers of Fumiko Ohkusa, who knew him in Hiroshima.】

-Mr. Omar was fair, with bright eyes and very likeable.

-He often sang an Indonesian song of that time called

" U sa sayage " with everyone.

I met with many kind people

when I went to Japan.

I am going back home now.

I will surely come back.

【Letter to Ms. Chieko Sasaki in Kyoto, 1945】

August 6, 1945

An event that lasted only a few seconds

Blew out the fire of life of millions

My life and all the rest

And my precious friends --

In that one second,

we were led into a pitch black world.

No treatment was available.

We were left to die in the grasslands.

The summer grass was burnt and looked like autumn grass.

Small birds, their wings burned off and unable to fly were walking on the grass.

Our clothing was in tatters.

Skin that was exposed was blistered and my face was abnormally enlarged.

The cruelly wounded, walked around like sleepwalkers.

【The devastation of Hiroshima immediately after exposure
                    to radiation : Dr. Tetsuo Hiratsuka's account.】

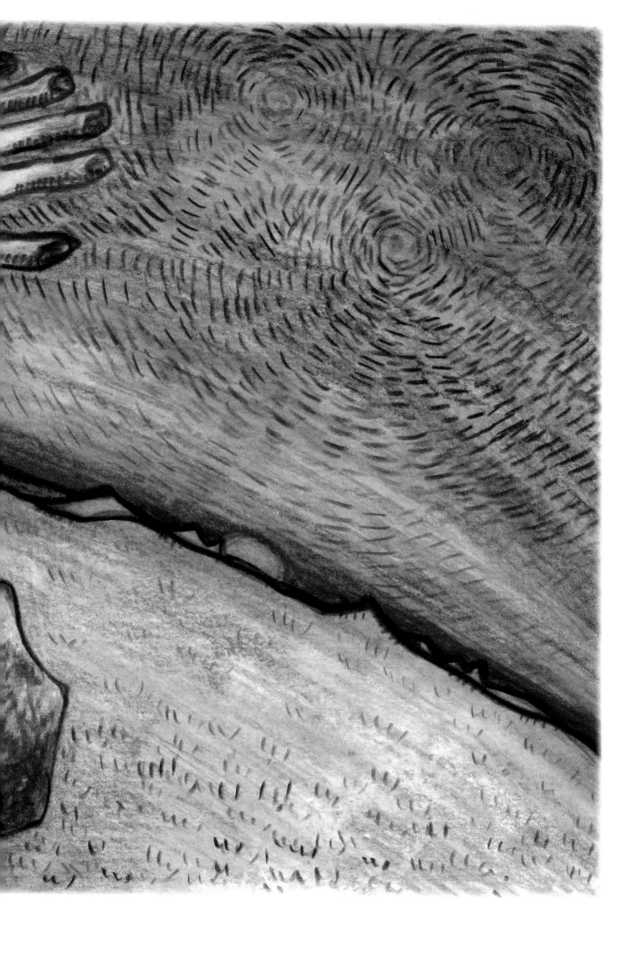

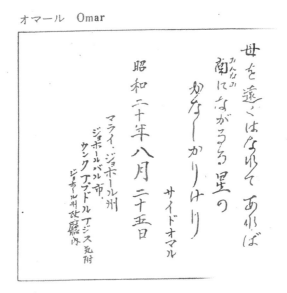

オマール　Omar

『 As my mother is far away, the stars that fall to the south would be sad 』

～ Prince Omar to Dr. Hamashima ～

【Omar's doctor at Kyoto University Hospital:

According to Dr. Yoshihiro Hamashima】

He was very weak. I remember it was the 28th of August, right after the turmoil at the end of the war, and his name was Said, Said Omar... Said meaning Prince -- he was very handsome.

We didn't know what to do for him, especially us !

I injected 200 cc of my blood twice a day. Prince Omar smiled and said,

"Oh, I feel so much better, I'm now your little brother, I have your blood in my veins, and I will never hate Japan."

Sept. 1945   Said Omar died in Kyoto

"The last view I saw was of a pitch black world."

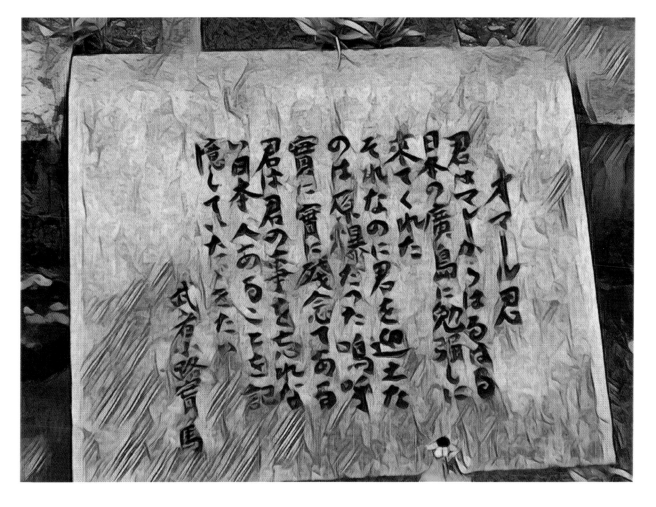

【Omar's Tomb】

You came all the way from Malaysia to study in Hiroshima, Japan. And yet you were greeted by an atomic bomb. I am truly, truly sorry. Please remember that we Japanese will never forget you.

--Mushanokouji Saneatsu

In June 1943, during the Greater East Asia War, Said Omar came to Japan as one of the special foreign students to the south at the request of the then Tojo Military Cabinet. He was from a prominent family in Johor, Malaysia, an ally of the Greater East Asia Co-prosperity Sphere and his outstanding qualities carried great expectations for his people.

While a student at Hiroshima University, Omar was exposed to the atomic bomb, and on his way back to Tokyo, he got off the train in Kyoto and was hospitalized at Kyoto University Hospital, but died a week later without any medical attention.

He was 18 years old. (Enko-ji Temple) and was buried at the time in Kyoto.

On September 3, 1961, on the anniversary of his death, an Islamic-style tombstone was erected with the cooperation of well-meaning citizens. (Kenkichi Sonobe, Yase Heihachi Tea House)

The Konan Dormitory was destroyed

by an atomic bomb on August 6, 1945.

【The Special Exchange Student Program in the South】

In 1942, students from the occupied territories in the south were invited to study abroad for the purpose of promoting the Greater East Asia Co-prosperity Sphere.

In a sense, they were also called "hostages". They received preparatory education in Tokyo and were educated at universities around the country.

Five students from the Konan dormitory were killed in the bombing of Hiroshima, and the survivors have been active in various fields since their return to Japan.

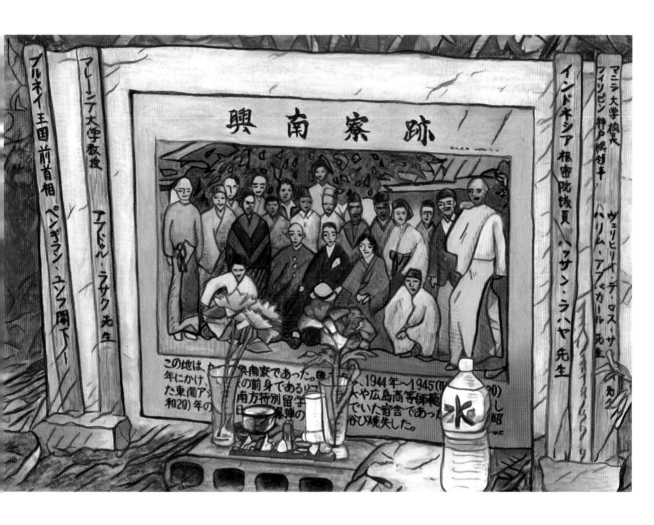

Photo taken on Sept. 20, 1944

His Royal Highness Pengiran Yusof, former Prime Minister of the Kingdom of Brunei

Dr. Hatsan Rahaya, Member of the Indonesian Privy Council

Dr. Abdul Razak, Professor, University of Malaysia

Since Hiroshima/Nagasaki,

more than 2038 nuclear tests have been

carried out.

Did they not learn from Hiroshima and Nagasaki ?

The illusion we believed we saw continue

to take away lives. "Peaceful use of nuclear

energy, nuclear power" ? ?

"There will be no immediate impact."

Who will believe in such words !

【Hiroshima Municipal High School

for Girls Cenotaph for the A-bomb Victims】

$E=MC^2$

This is Einstein's theory of relativity, "Energy equals mass times the speed of light squared" which expresses the equivalence of mass and energy.

It became the principle for the atomic bomb. And was used during the Allied Occupation when the words "atomic bomb" could not be used.

【Kyoto University Research Reactor Institute: Dr. Tetsuji Imanaka】
Spent nuclear fuel from nuclear power plants produces plutonium, in fact, the opposite is true. The nuclear reactors were originally built to extract plutonium to make atomic bombs. It was originally a bomb. Nuclear weapons and nuclear power plants are connected at the root.

The technology for making nuclear power plants came out of the development of atomic bombs, and they are the same in origin.

The number of nuclear power plants is increasing, and we are forcing the next generation to deal with the nonprocessable waste.Prometheus gave fire to mankind. Mankind receive many benefits based on fire including civilization and technology but at the same time, it also used that fire to create weapons and start wars. And it became a terrible fire that consumed everything.

~ From Greek Mythology ~

If we continue as such, every second brings us

closer to the world of darkness.

May you give the human race,

wisdom and hope !

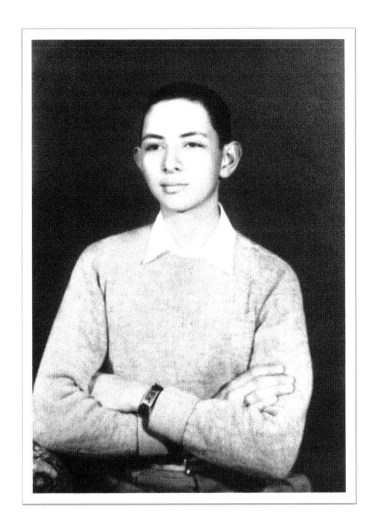

Epilogue

   I, Hirokazu Furuta, used to visit the grave once a year at Enko-ji Temple in Kyoto City.
When I was in my early elementary school years, I asked my relatives about unusual graves. I could not read the kanji and did not understand the meaning, but by the time I was in the first year of junior high school, I began to understand most of the meanings. I had heard that my grandfather had suffered a very frightening atomic bombing in Hiroshima, so I was drawn to Mr. Omar's grave.

   After I turned 40, I had a meeting with Dr. Tetsuo Hiratsuka, a senior dentist (I knew he was 85 years old at the time and president of the Kyoto A-bomb Survivors Association), and we talked about the A-bomb and Omar's grave. At that time, as the mystery was solved and I learned more details, I felt that this must be passed on to future generations, and I decided to ask Dr. Tetsuo Hiratsuka for his records and stories while he was still alive.

I received materials and was preparing to follow in the footsteps of Mr. Omar, a special student from the South, and record the horror of the atomic bombing. While I was photographing various locations, the accident at the Fukushima Daiichi Nuclear Power Plant caused by the Great East Japan Earthquake on March 11, 2011 brought further radiation damage and nuclear threats to Japan. The more I researched, the more I realized the horror of nuclear power plants, so I dared to shoot on location in Fukushima. We then produced a documentary film, "Hiroshima is crying, Fukushima is crying," with interviews with the people involved, in order to appeal for peace and nuclear abolition. In addition, to make this story known to the world, even if just a little bit,

I wanted to tell this story to future generations in the form of a picture book.
We would also like to translate the story into English so that it can be told in Malaysia and other countries.

 Original draft : "Hiroshima is Crying" by Tetsuo Hiratsuka / Script by Atsuki Ueshima / Cooperation: Professor Emeritus, Kyoto University, Kyoto, Japan / Cooperation: Yoshihiro Hamashima, Professor Emeritus of Kyoto University, former President of Kyoto Women's University / Tetsuo Hiratsuka, Chairman of Kyoto A-bomb Survivors' Association, Former Chairman of Kyoto Dental Association / CG production: Atsuko Mimura

 Compiled by : Hirokazu Furuta
Born in Osaka, lives in Kyoto / Dentist and film and theater producer / Directed the documentary film "Hiroshima is Crying, Fukushima is Crying" and has been involved in numerous theater and film productions.

 Picture by : Asuka Fujiwara
Living in Kyoto City/Graduated from Kyoto Seika University Faculty of Fine Arts / Main vocalist and sanshin player of the music unit Tui Titi

 English translation : Yoko Narahashi
Director, film director, playwright, lyricist, English conversation educator, casting director, Representative of "UPS ACADEMY", a training school for actors who can play an active role in the world. She graduated from International Christian University（ICU）.

オマール王子の旅 ～広島で原爆に遭った南方特別留学生～ （英訳）

2023 年 9 月 1 日　初版　第 1 刷　発行　　　　　　　定価はカバーに表示しています。

作	古田　博一
絵	藤原　飛鳥
英訳	奈良橋　陽子
発行所	（株）あいり出版
	〒600-8436 京都市下京区室町通松原下る元両替町 259-1 ベラジオ五条烏丸 305
	TEL ／ FAX　075-344-4505　http://airpub.jp/
発行者	石黒　憲一
印刷／製本	日本ハイコム（株）

装丁・ブックデザイン　竹岡 紀子　　　© 2023　ISBN978-4-86555-112-9 C8795 Printed in Japan